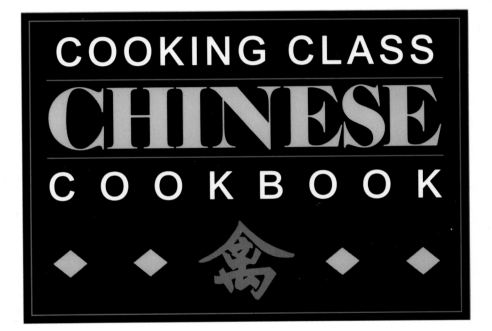

# COOKING CLASS
# CHINESE
# COOKBOOK

PUBLICATIONS INTERNATIONAL, LTD.

ISBN: 1-56173-986-3

**Pictured on the front cover:** Kung Pao Chicken (*page 58*).
**Pictured on the inside front cover:** Shrimp Toast (*page 10*).
**Pictured on the back cover:** Hors d'Oeuvre Rolls (*page 15*).

8 7 6 5 4 3 2 1

Manufactured in the U.S.A.

# CONTENTS

CLASS NOTES
6

APPETIZERS & SOUPS
10

VEGETABLE DISHES
26

MEATS
34

POULTRY
55

FISH & SEAFOOD
74

RICE & NOODLES
88

INDEX
94

Long Soup (*page 18*)

Beef with Peppers (*page 48*)

Chicken with Lychees (*page 66*)

# CLASS NOTES

## TECHNIQUES FOR CHINESE COOKING

Preparing tasty and attractive Chinese dishes can be a rewarding experience that is easy to accomplish. There are just a few rules to keep in mind for successfully cooking most recipes: 1) Preparation and cooking are two separate procedures. 2) All ingredients should be prepared *before* any cooking is begun. 3) Paying attention to the cooking process is crucial because many of the foods are cooked over intense heat in a matter of minutes.

The Chinese have perfected a variety of cooking techniques, including stir-frying, deep-frying, braising, stewing, steaming, roasting, barbecuing and preserving. All of these techniques are probably familiar to you. But in order to stir-fry correctly, an understanding of its basic principles is necessary.

Stir-frying—a rapid-cooking method invented by the Chinese—is the brisk cooking of small pieces of ingredients in hot oil over intense heat for a short time, usually just for a few minutes. During cooking, the ingredients must be kept in constant motion by stirring or tossing vigorously. Once cooking is completed, the food should be removed immediately from heat.

When stir-frying, all of the ingredients must be well organized and prepared *before the cooking is started.* They should be measured or weighed, cleaned, chopped, sliced, combined or the like. Meat, poultry, fish and vegetables should be cut into pieces of approximately the same size for even cooking. Otherwise, one ingredient may be overcooked while others remain undercooked. The stir-frying is accomplished so quickly that there is usually not time to complete any preparation steps once cooking is begun.

The intensity of the heat used for stir-frying is important. In most cases, easily controlled high heat is needed. For this reason, a gas range with its ability for instant heat control is generally more efficient for stir-frying than is an electric range.

The kind of oil used is also crucial. A vegetable oil that can be heated to a high temperature without smoking is essential. Peanut oil, corn oil, cottonseed oil and soybean oil all work well. Other kinds of fats, such as olive oil, sesame oil, butter or lard cannot be used because they have low burning points.

Due to the variables involved in stir-frying, such as kinds of foods, type of heat and the kind of cooking equipment used, cooking times given in this publication should be used as guidelines—not as absolutes. Most of the recipes, for example, were tested on a gas range. Cooking times needed when using a wok on an electric range, or when using an electric wok, may vary somewhat.

## UTENSILS FOR CHINESE COOKING

A reasonably equipped kitchen usually contains more than enough utensils to adequately handle Chinese cooking. However, one item you may not have, but may wish to consider purchasing, is a wok, especially if you plan to make stir-fried dishes often. Invented many centuries ago, the wok is an all-purpose cooking pan used in virtually every Chinese household for almost every kind of cooking.

Traditionally, a wok was made from thin, tempered iron, and had a rounded bottom for fast, even conduction of heat. However, modern technology has brought some changes to the wok. In addition to iron, woks are now manufactured in aluminum, stainless steel and carbon steel. Woks with flat bottoms are made for use on electric ranges and on smooth-top cooking surfaces. There are electric woks with nonstick finishes and automatic thermostatic controls. On some woks, the customary thin metal handles positioned on two sides have been replaced with a single long wooden handle. This version eliminates the necessity of keeping pot holders handy at all times to pick up or steady the wok.

Woks range in size from 12 to 24 inches in diameter. The 14-inch size is a good choice because it can handle most stir-frying and other cooking chores without interfering with the use of other burners on the range top.

Before a new iron or carbon steel wok is used, it should be washed and seasoned. Wash it thoroughly in hot, soapy water (the first time only) and use a scouring pad, if necessary, to remove any protective coating. Rinse the wok with water and dry it completely. Rub 1 tablespoon of vegetable oil completely over the interior of the wok. Place it over low heat until hot throughout, 3 to 5 minutes; remove wok from heat and let cool.

After each use, the wok should be soaked in hot water and cleaned with a bamboo brush or a sponge. Do not clean the wok with soap or soap-treated scouring pads. Rinse the wok with water, dry it and place over low heat until all water evaporates. Then rub 1 teaspoon of vegetable oil over the inside of the wok to prevent it from rusting.

Another very useful utensil for Chinese cooking is a cleaver. While not essential, it is handy for slicing, chopping and mincing ingredients, and is especially helpful for chopping whole chickens into Chinese-style serving pieces (see page 55).

## INGREDIENTS IN CHINESE CUISINE

When preparing Chinese foods, you will come across many ingredients that are familiar. You will also encounter some that may be unfamiliar such as wood ears, oyster sauce or Chinese five-spice powder. Some of the items—seasonings in particular—may be available only in Chinese food markets. Before you search for an out-of-the-way specialty store, however, check your local supermarket. Many supermarkets now stock good inventories of Chinese ingredients. In addition to canned, bottled or packaged goods, many carry fresh items such as Chinese cabbage (napa or bok choy), bean sprouts, wonton and egg-roll wrappers, bean curd and Chinese-style thin egg noodles. A check of the frozen-food cases will yield additional Chinese items.

As with any other kind of cooking, choose the freshest ingredients you can find, especially when purchasing vegetables, meat, poultry or fish. The Chinese are so conscientious about cooking with the freshest possible foods that they plan their menus around the foods they find in the market—rather than planning the marketing around the menu.

The glossary that follows describes many of the Chinese foods used in the recipes in this publication.

## GLOSSARY OF CHINESE INGREDIENTS

**Bamboo shoots:** tender, ivory-colored shoots of tropical bamboo plants, used separately as a vegetable and to add crispness and a slight sweetness to dishes. They are available in cans—whole or sliced—and should be rinsed with water before using.

**Bean curd** (also called tofu): puréed soybeans pressed to form a white custard-like cake, used as a vegetable and as an excellent source of protein. Bean curd can be used in all kinds of recipes because it readily absorbs the flavor of other foods. Bean curd is available fresh or in cans. If fresh, it should be covered with water and stored in the refrigerator.

**Bean sauce** (also called yellow bean sauce or brown bean sauce): a Chinese seasoning made from soybeans, flour, vinegar, salt and spices such as hot chilies.

**Bean sprouts:** small white shoots of the pea-like mung bean plant, used separately as a vegetable and included in a wide variety of dishes. They are available fresh or in cans. Canned sprouts should be rinsed before use to eliminate any metallic taste. Fresh or opened, unused canned sprouts should be covered with water and stored in the refrigerator.

**Bean threads** (also called Chinese rice vermicelli, transparent or cellophane noodles): dry, hard, white, fine noodles made from powdered mung beans. They have little flavor of their own, but readily absorb the flavors of other foods. Bean threads can be used in numerous steamed, simmered, deep-fried or stir-fried dishes. They are available in packets or small bundles.

**Cabbage, Chinese:** there are two types of Chinese cabbages generally available in American markets. One is bok choy, which has white stalks and green, crinkled leaves. The other is napa cabbage which has elongated tightly furled leaves with wide white ribs and soft pale green tips. Both varieties need very little cooking and are often included in soups and stir-fried dishes.

**Chili oil** (also called chili pepper oil or hot pepper oil): reddish colored, fiery hot oil made from peanut oil infused with dried red chili peppers. Use sparingly for flavoring. Store in cool, dark place.

**Chili sauce, Chinese:** a bright red, extremely spicy sauce made from crushed fresh chili peppers and salt. It is available in cans or bottles and should be used sparingly.

**Chives, Chinese** (also called garlic chives): thin, slender, flat green leaves give a distinctive garlic flavor to many Chinese dishes.

**Corn, baby:** 2- to 3-inch long yellow ears of corn with tiny kernels. The edible cobs are slightly sweet tasting and crunchy. Available in cans or jars packed in salted water, drain or rinse with cold water to remove brine before using. Store, covered with water in jar, in refrigerator up to 1½ weeks; change water every 2 days.

**Egg noodles, Chinese-style:** thin pasta usually made of flour, egg, water and salt. The noodles can be purchased fresh, frozen or dehydrated. They can be boiled, braised, stir-fried or deep-fried; the time and method of cooking vary with the type of noodle. Check the package for specific instructions.

**Five-spice powder, Chinese:** cocoa-colored, ready-mixed blend of five ground spices, usually anise seed, fennel, clove, cinnamon and ginger or pepper. It has a slightly sweet, pungent flavor and should be used sparingly.

**Ginger** (also called ginger root): a knobby, gnarled root, having a brown skin and whitish or light green interior. It has a fresh, pungent flavor and is used as a basic seasoning in many Chinese recipes. Ginger is available fresh or in cans. It will keep for weeks in the refrigerator wrapped in plastic, or for months if kept in salted water or dry sherry. Always remove the outer brown skin from fresh ginger before using in any recipe.

**Hoisin sauce:** a thick, dark brown sauce made of soybeans, flour, sugar, spices, garlic, chili and salt. It has a sweet, spicy flavor and is called for in numerous Chinese recipes.

**Lychee** (also called lichee or litchi): a small, juicy, oval-shaped fruit with a brownish or bright red skin, white pulp and large pit. It is used in main dishes in combination with other foods or served separately as a dessert or snack. Lychees are available in cans whole, pitted and packed in syrup.

**Mushrooms, dried:** dehydrated black or brown mushrooms from the Orient, having caps from 1 to 3 inches in diameter. They have a strong, distinctive flavor and are included in many different kinds of recipes. Chinese dried mushrooms must be soaked in hot water before using; they are usually thinly sliced prior to combining them with other foods. Dried mushrooms are available in cellophane packages.

**Oyster sauce:** a thick, brown, concentrated sauce made of ground oysters, soy sauce and brine. It imparts very little fish flavor and is used as a seasoning to intensify other flavors. Oyster sauce is included in a variety of recipes, especially in stir-fried Cantonese dishes.

**Parsley, Chinese** (also called cilantro or fresh coriander): a strongly flavored green herb with flat broad leaves similar in appearance to Italian or flat-leaf parsley. Commonly used fresh as a seasoning or garnish.

**Plum sauce:** a thick, piquant chutney-like sauce frequently served with duck or pork dishes. It is available in cans or bottles.

**Satay (Saté) sauce** (also called Chinese barbecue sauce): a dark brown, hot, spicy sauce composed of soy sauce, ground shrimp, chili peppers, sugar, garlic, oil and spices. It is available in cans or jars.

**Sesame oil:** an amber-colored oil pressed from toasted sesame seeds. It has a strong, nut-like flavor and is best used sparingly. Sesame oil is generally used as a flavoring, not as a cooking oil because of its low smoking point. It is available in bottles.

**Snow peas:** (also called pea pods or Chinese peas): flat, green pods that are picked before the peas have matured. They add crispness, color and flavor to foods, require very little cooking and are frequently used in stir-fried dishes. Snow peas are available fresh or frozen.

**Soy sauce:** a pungent, brown, salty liquid made of fermented soybeans, wheat, yeast, salt and, sometimes, sugar. It is an essential ingredient in Chinese cooking. There are several types of soy sauces (light, dark, heavy), as well as Japanese-style soy sauce. The Japanese style sauce is somewhere between light and dark varieties. All types of soy sauce are available in bottles.

**Szechuan (Sichuan) peppercorns:** a reddish-brown pepper with a strong, pungent aroma and flavor with a time-delayed action—its potent flavor may not be noticed immediately. It should be used sparingly. It is usually sold whole or crushed in small packages.

**Vinegar, rice:** a light, mellow and mildly tangy vinegar brewed from rice. Do not use brands that are not brewed or that are seasoned with salt and sugar. Cider vinegar can be used as a substitution for rice vinegar, except when preparing sushi rice. Store in a cool, dark place.

**Water chestnut:** a walnut-sized bulb from an aquatic plant. The bulb has a tough, brown skin and crisp white interior. Water chestnuts are served separately as a vegetable and are used to add crisp texture and delicate sweet flavor to dishes. They are available fresh or in cans.

**Wonton wrappers:** commercially prepared dough that is rolled thinly and cut into 3- to 4-inch squares. They are available fresh or frozen.

**Wood ears** (also called tree ears or cloud ears): a dried fungus that expands to five or six times its dehydrated size when soaked in warm water. They have a delicate flavor and crunchy texture and are most often used in soups. They are available in cellophane packages.

# Shrimp Toast

12 large shrimp, shelled and
   deveined, leaving tails intact
1 egg
2½ tablespoons cornstarch
¼ teaspoon salt
   Dash of pepper
3 slices white sandwich bread,
   crusts removed and quartered
1 slice cooked ham, cut into
   ½-inch pieces
1 hard-cooked egg yolk, cut into
   ½-inch pieces
1 green onion with top, finely
   chopped
   Vegetable oil for frying
   Hard-cooked egg half and
   Green Onion Curls (page 22)
   for garnish

1. Cut deep slit down back of each shrimp; press gently with fingers to flatten.

2. Beat raw egg, cornstarch, salt and pepper in large bowl until blended. Add shrimp; toss to coat well.

3. Place one shrimp, cut-side down, on each bread piece; press shrimp gently into bread.

4. Brush small amount of egg mixture over each shrimp.

5. Place one piece *each* of ham and egg yolk and a scant ¼ teaspoon onion on top of each shrimp.

6. Heat oil in wok or large skillet over medium-high heat to 375°F. Add three or four bread pieces at a time; cook until golden, 1 to 2 minutes on each side. Drain on paper towels. Garnish, if desired.          *Makes 1 dozen*

Step 1. Flattening shrimp

Step 4. Brushing egg mixture over shrimp.

Step 5. Placing egg yolk on shrimp.

# Pot Stickers

2 cups all-purpose flour
¾ cup *plus* 2 tablespoons boiling
   water
½ cup very finely chopped napa
   cabbage
8 ounces lean ground pork
1 green onion with top, finely
   chopped
2 tablespoons finely chopped
   water chestnuts
1½ teaspoons soy sauce
1½ teaspoons dry sherry
1½ teaspoons cornstarch
½ teaspoon minced fresh ginger
½ teaspoon sesame oil
¼ teaspoon sugar
2 tablespoons vegetable oil,
   divided
⅔ cup chicken broth, divided
   Soy sauce, vinegar and chili oil

1. Place flour in large bowl; make well in center. Pour in boiling water; stir with wooden spoon until mixture forms dough.

2. Place dough on lightly floured surface; flatten slightly. To knead dough, fold dough in half toward you and press dough away from you with heel of hand. Give dough a quarter turn and continue folding, pushing and turning. Continue kneading 5 minutes or until smooth and elastic, adding additional flour to prevent sticking if necessary. Wrap dough in plastic wrap; let stand 30 minutes.

3. For filling, squeeze cabbage to remove as much moisture as possible; place in large bowl. Add pork, onion, water chestnuts, soy sauce, sherry, cornstarch, ginger, sesame oil and sugar; mix well.

4. Unwrap dough and knead briefly (as described in step 2) on lightly floured surface; divide into two equal pieces. Cover one piece with plastic wrap or clean towel while working with other piece.

5. Using lightly floured rolling pin, roll out dough to ⅛-inch thickness on lightly floured surface.

6. Cut out 3-inch circles with round cookie cutter or top of clean empty can.

7. Place 1 rounded teaspoon filling in center of each dough circle.

*continued on page 14*

Step 1. Stirring flour mixture to form dough.

Step 2. Kneading dough.

Step 6. Cutting out dough circles.

8. To shape each pot sticker, lightly moisten edge of one dough circle with water; fold in half.

9. Starting at one end, pinch curled edges together making four pleats along edge; set pot sticker down firmly, seam-side up. Cover finished pot stickers with plastic wrap while shaping remaining pot stickers.

10. Pot stickers may be cooked immediately or covered securely and stored in refrigerator up to 4 hours. Pot stickers may also be frozen. To freeze, place pot stickers on cookie sheet or shallow pan; place in freezer 30 minutes to firm slightly. Remove from freezer; place in freezer-weight resealable plastic bag. Freeze up to 3 months. (Frozen pot stickers do not need to be thawed before cooking.)

11. To cook pot stickers, heat 1 tablespoon vegetable oil in large nonstick skillet over medium heat. Place 1/2 of pot stickers in skillet, seam-side up. Cook until bottoms are golden brown, 5 to 6 minutes.

12. Pour in 1/3 cup chicken broth; cover tightly. Reduce heat to low. Simmer until all liquid is absorbed, about 10 minutes (15 minutes if frozen). Repeat with remaining vegetable oil, pot stickers and chicken broth.

13. Place pot stickers on serving platter. Serve with soy sauce, vinegar and chili oil for dipping.

*Makes about 3 dozen*

Step 8. Shaping pot stickers.

Step 9. Pleating pot stickers.

Step 11. Browning pot stickers.

# Hors d'Oeuvre Rolls

Sweet and Sour Sauce (recipe follows on page 16), optional
8 ounces deveined shelled shrimp (page 74)
1 package (17¼ ounces) frozen ready-to-bake puff pastry sheets *or* 40 wonton wrappers
½ cup Chinese-style thin egg noodles, broken into 1-inch pieces
2 tablespoons butter or margarine
4 ounces boneless lean pork, finely chopped
6 fresh medium mushrooms, finely chopped
6 green onions with tops, finely chopped
1 hard-cooked egg, finely chopped
1½ tablespoons dry sherry
½ teaspoon salt
⅛ teaspoon pepper
1 egg, lightly beaten
Vegetable oil for frying
Vegetable bundle* for garnish

*To make vegetable bundle, cut 6- to 8-inch length off top of green onion. Place in salted water; let stand at least 15 minutes. Tie around small bundle of fresh vegetables.

1. Prepare Sweet and Sour Sauce.

2. Place enough water to cover shrimp in medium saucepan. Bring to a boil over medium-high heat. Add shrimp. Reduce heat to low. Simmer 5 to 10 minutes or until shrimp curl and turn pink. (Do not overcook shrimp as they will become tough.) Drain and set aside to cool.

3. Remove puff pastry from freezer. Let stand, uncovered, at room temperature until ready to use, about 20 minutes.

4. Meanwhile, cook noodles according to package directions just until tender but still firm, 2 to 3 minutes. Drain and rinse under cold running water; drain again. Chop noodles finely.

5. Heat butter in wok or large skillet over medium-high heat. Add pork; stir-fry until no longer pink in center, about 5 minutes.

6. Add mushrooms and onions; stir-fry 2 minutes.

7. Remove wok from heat. Finely chop shrimp. Add to wok with noodles, hard-cooked egg, sherry, salt and pepper; mix well.

8. If using puff pastry, gently unfold each pastry sheet. If pastry is too soft, place it in refrigerator for a few minutes to chill. For ease in handling, pastry should be cold to the touch. Place pastry on lightly floured surface. With lightly floured rolling pin, roll and trim each sheet to 15 × 12-inch rectangle; cut into twenty (3-inch) squares.

Step 4. Chopping noodles.

Step 5. Stir-frying pork.

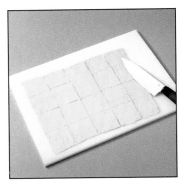
Step 8. Cutting out dough squares.

*continued on page 16*

9. Spoon 1 tablespoon pork mixture across center of each pastry square or wonton wrapper.

10. Brush edges lightly with beaten egg. Roll up tightly around filling; pinch edges slightly to seal.

11. Heat oil in wok or large skillet to 375°F. Add four to six rolls at a time; cook until golden and crisp, 3 to 5 minutes. Drain on paper towels. Garnish, if desired. Serve with Sweet and Sour Sauce.          *Makes 40 rolls*

# Sweet and Sour Sauce

**4 teaspoons cornstarch**
**1 cup water**
**$1/2$ cup distilled white vinegar**
**$1/2$ cup sugar**
**$1/4$ cup tomato paste**

Combine all ingredients in small saucepan. Bring to a boil over medium heat, stirring constantly. Boil 1 minute, stirring constantly. Set aside until ready to use or cover and refrigerate up to 8 hours.

Step 9. Spooning filling onto dough.

Step 10. Rolling up dough.

Step 11. Cooking rolls.

# Long Soup

¹/₄ of small head of cabbage
   (4 to 6 ounces)
1¹/₂ tablespoons vegetable oil
  8 ounces boneless lean pork, cut
   into thin strips
  6 cups chicken broth
  2 tablespoons soy sauce
¹/₂ teaspoon minced fresh ginger
  4 ounces Chinese-style thin egg
   noodles
  8 green onions with tops,
   diagonally cut into ¹/₂-inch
   slices

1. Remove core from cabbage; discard.

2. Shred cabbage.

3. Heat oil in wok or large skillet over medium-high heat. Add cabbage and pork; stir-fry until pork is no longer pink in center, about 5 minutes.

4. Add chicken broth, soy sauce and ginger. Bring to a boil. Reduce heat to low; simmer 10 minutes, stirring occasionally. Stir in onions.

5. Add noodles.

6. Cook just until noodles are tender, 2 to 4 minutes. *Makes 4 servings*

Step 1. Removing core from cabbage.

Step 5. Adding noodles to wok.

Step 6. Cooking noodles.

# Stuffed Mushrooms

24 fresh medium mushrooms
(about 1 pound)
6 ounces boneless lean pork
¼ cup whole water chestnuts
(¼ of 8-ounce can)
3 green onions with tops
½ small red or green pepper
1 small stalk celery
1 teaspoon cornstarch
1 teaspoon minced fresh ginger
2 teaspoons dry sherry
1 teaspoon soy sauce
½ teaspoon hoisin sauce
1 egg white, lightly beaten
Vegetable oil for frying
Batter (recipe follows)
½ cup all-purpose flour
Fresh thyme leaves for garnish

1. Clean mushrooms by wiping with damp paper towel.

2. Remove stems from mushrooms; set caps aside. Chop stems finely; transfer to large bowl.

3. Finely chop pork, water chestnuts, onions, red pepper and celery. Add to chopped mushroom stems. Add cornstarch, ginger, sherry, soy sauce, hoisin sauce and egg white; mix well.

4. Spoon pork mixture into mushroom caps, mounding slightly in center.

5. Heat oil in wok or large skillet over high heat to 375°F. Meanwhile, prepare Batter.

6. Dip mushrooms into flour, then into batter, coating completely.

7. Add six to eight mushrooms to hot oil; cook until golden brown on all sides, about 5 minutes. Drain on paper towels. Repeat with remaining mushrooms. Garnish, if desired.

*Makes 2 dozen*

Step 1. Cleaning mushrooms.

Step 4. Stuffing mushroom caps.

## Batter

½ cup cornstarch
½ cup all-purpose flour
1½ teaspoons baking powder
¾ teaspoon salt
⅓ cup milk
⅓ cup water

Combine cornstarch, flour, baking powder and salt in medium bowl. Add milk and water; beat with wire whisk until well blended.

Step 6. Coating stuffed mushrooms with flour and batter.

# Barbecued Pork

1/4 cup soy sauce
2 tablespoons dry red wine
1 tablespoon packed brown sugar
1 tablespoon honey
2 teaspoons red food coloring
   (optional)
1/2 teaspoon ground cinnamon
1 green onion with top, cut in half
1 clove garlic, minced
2 whole pork tenderloins (about
   12 ounces *each*), trimmed
   Green Onion Curls (recipe
   follows) for garnish

1. Combine soy sauce, wine, sugar, honey, food coloring, cinnamon, onion and garlic in large bowl. Add meat; turn to coat completely. Cover and refrigerate 1 hour or overnight, turning meat occasionally.

2. Preheat oven to 350°F. Drain meat, reserving marinade. Place meat on wire rack over baking pan. Bake 45 minutes or until no longer pink in center, turning and basting frequently with reserved marinade.

3. Remove meat from oven; cool. Cut into diagonal slices. Garnish with Green Onion Curls, if desired.

*Makes about 8 appetizer servings*

## Green Onion Curls

6 to 8 medium green onions with tops
Cold water
10 to 12 ice cubes

1. Trim bulbs (white part) from onions; reserve for another use. Trim remaining stems (green part) to 4-inch lengths.

2. Using sharp scissors, cut each section of green stems lengthwise into very thin strips down to beginning of stems, cutting six to eight strips in each stem section.

3. Fill large bowl about half full with cold water. Add green onions and ice cubes. Refrigerate until onions curl, about 1 hour; drain.

*Makes 6 to 8 curls*

Green Onion Curls: Step 1.
Trimming onions.

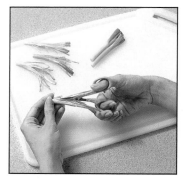

Green Onion Curls: Step 2.
Cutting onion stems into strips.

Green Onion Curls: Step 3.
Soaking onions.

# Wonton Soup

½ cup finely chopped cabbage
8 ounces lean ground pork
4 ounces deveined shelled shrimp, finely chopped
3 green onions with tops, finely chopped
1 egg, lightly beaten
1½ tablespoons cornstarch
2 teaspoons soy sauce
2 teaspoons sesame oil, divided
1 teaspoon oyster sauce
48 wonton wrappers (about 1 pound)
1 egg white, lightly beaten
¾ pound bok choy *or* napa cabbage
6 cups chicken broth
1 cup thinly sliced Barbecued Pork (page 22)
3 green onions with tops, thinly sliced
Edible flowers for garnish

1. For filling, squeeze cabbage to remove as much moisture as possible. Place cabbage in large bowl. Add pork, shrimp, chopped onions, whole egg, cornstarch, soy sauce, 1½ teaspoons sesame oil and oyster sauce; mix well.

2. For wontons, work with about twelve wrappers at a time, keeping remaining wrappers covered with plastic wrap. Place one wonton wrapper on work surface with one point facing you. Place 1 teaspoon filling in bottom corner; fold bottom corner over filling.

3. Moisten side corners of wonton wrapper with egg white. Bring side corners together, overlapping slightly; pinch together firmly to seal. Cover finished wontons with plastic wrap while filling remaining wontons. (Cook immediately, refrigerate up to 8 hours or freeze in resealable plastic bag.)

4. Add wontons to large pot of boiling water; cook until filling is no longer pink, about 4 minutes (6 minutes if frozen); drain. Place in bowl of cold water to prevent wontons from sticking together.

5. Cut bok choy stems into 1-inch slices; cut leaves in half crosswise. Set aside.

6. Bring chicken broth to a boil in large saucepan. Add bok choy and remaining ½ teaspoon sesame oil; simmer 2 minutes. Drain wontons; add to hot broth. Add slices of Barbecued Pork and sliced onions. Ladle into soup bowls. Serve immediately. Garnish, if desired. *Makes 6 servings*

Step 2. Folding wonton wrapper over filling.

Step 3. Shaping wontons.

# Chinese Vegetables

2 medium yellow onions
1 pound fresh broccoli*
8 ounces fresh snow peas *or*
    1 package (6 ounces) thawed
    frozen snow peas*
3/4 cup water
1 tablespoon instant chicken
    bouillon granules
2 tablespoons vegetable oil
1 tablespoon minced fresh ginger
8 ounces fresh spinach,* coarsely
    chopped
4 stalks celery,* diagonally cut
    into 1/2-inch pieces
8 green onions with tops,*
    diagonally cut into thin slices

*Or, use sliced carrots, zucchini, green beans or green peppers in addition to, or in place of, the listed vegetables.

1. Cut yellow onions into eight wedges; separate layers (page 64).

2. Trim woody stems from broccoli; discard.

3. Cut broccoli tops into florets.

4. Cut larger florets and stalks into $2 \times 1/4$-inch strips; set aside.

5. Trim snow peas and remove strings; set aside.

6. Combine water and bouillon granules in small bowl; mix well. Set aside.

7. Heat oil in wok or large skillet over high heat. Add yellow onions, broccoli strips and ginger; stir-fry 1 minute. Add broccoli florets, snow peas, spinach, celery and green onions; toss lightly.

8. Add bouillon mixture; mix lightly until vegetables are well coated. Bring to a boil; cover. Cook until vegetables are crisp-tender, 2 to 3 minutes. *Makes 4 to 6 servings*

Step 3. Cutting broccoli into florets.

Step 4. Cutting larger florets and stalks into strips.

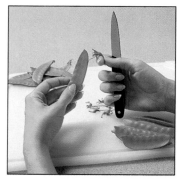

Step 5. Trimming snow peas.

# Zucchini Shanghai Style

4 dried mushrooms
  Water
1 large tomato
½ cup chicken broth
2 tablespoons ketchup
2 teaspoons soy sauce
1 teaspoon dry sherry
¼ teaspoon sugar
⅛ teaspoon salt
1 teaspoon red wine vinegar
1 teaspoon cornstarch
2 tablespoons vegetable oil,
  divided
1 teaspoon minced fresh ginger
1 clove garlic, minced
1 green onion with top, finely
  chopped
1 pound zucchini, diagonally cut
  into 1-inch pieces
½ small yellow onion, cut into
  wedges and separated

1. Place mushrooms in small bowl; add enough warm water to cover mushrooms completely. Let stand 30 minutes. Drain, reserving ¼ cup liquid. Squeeze out excess water.

2. Cut stems off mushrooms; discard. Cut caps into thin slices.

3. To loosen skin from tomato, add tomato to small saucepan of boiling water. Let stand 30 to 45 seconds. Rinse immediately under cold running water. Gently peel skin from tomato.

4. Cut tomato in half. Remove stem and seeds; discard.

5. Coarsely chop tomato; set aside.

6. Combine reserved ¼ cup mushroom liquid, chicken broth, ketchup, soy sauce, sherry, sugar, salt and vinegar in small bowl; set aside.

7. Combine cornstarch and 1 tablespoon water in small cup; mix well. Set aside.

8. Heat 1 tablespoon oil in wok or large skillet over medium-high heat. Add ginger and garlic; stir-fry 10 seconds. Add mushrooms, tomato and green onion; stir-fry 1 minute. Stir in chicken broth mixture. Bring to a boil. Reduce heat to low; simmer 10 minutes, stirring occasionally. Remove from wok; set aside.

9. Add remaining 1 tablespoon oil to wok; heat over medium-high heat. Add zucchini and yellow onion; stir-fry 30 seconds. Add 3 tablespoons water; cover. Cook, stirring occasionally, until vegetables are crisp-tender, 3 to 4 minutes. Add tomato mixture. Stir cornstarch mixture. Cook and stir until sauce boils and thickens.

*Makes 4 to 6 servings*

Step 3. Peeling tomato.

Step 4. Removing tomato seeds.

# Ma Po Bean Curd

1 tablespoon Szechuan
   peppercorns* (optional)
12 to 14 ounces bean curd, drained
3/4 cup chicken broth
1 tablespoon soy sauce
1 tablespoon dry sherry
1 1/2 tablespoons cornstarch
3 tablespoons water
2 tablespoons vegetable oil
4 ounces lean ground pork
2 teaspoons minced fresh ginger
2 cloves garlic, minced
1 tablespoon hot bean sauce
2 green onions with tops, thinly
   sliced
1 teaspoon sesame oil
   Fresh chives for garnish

*Szechuan peppercorns are deceptively
potent. Wear rubber or plastic gloves
when crushing them and do not touch
eyes or lips when handling.

1. Place peppercorns in small dry skillet. Cook and stir over medium-low heat until fragrant, about 2 minutes; let cool.

2. Place peppercorns between paper towels; crush with hammer. Set aside.

3. Cut bean curd into 1/2-inch cubes. Set aside.

4. Combine chicken broth, soy sauce and sherry in small bowl; set aside. Combine cornstarch and water in small cup; mix well. Set aside.

5. Heat vegetable oil in wok or large skillet over high heat. Add meat; stir-fry until no longer pink, about 2 minutes. Add ginger, garlic and hot bean sauce. Stir-fry until meat absorbs color from bean sauce, about 1 minute.

6. Add chicken broth mixture and bean curd; simmer, uncovered, 5 minutes. Stir in onions. Stir cornstarch mixture; add to wok. Cook until sauce boils and thickens slightly, stirring constantly. Stir in sesame oil. Sprinkle with ground peppercorns and garnish, if desired.

*Makes 3 to 4 servings*

Step 1. Cooking peppercorns.

Step 2. Crushing peppercorns.

Step 3. Cutting bean curd into cubes.

# *Chinese Mixed Pickled Vegetables*

**Pickling Liquid**
  3 cups sugar
  3 cups distilled white vinegar
1$\frac{1}{2}$ cups water
1$\frac{1}{2}$ teaspoons salt

**Vegetables**
  1 large Chinese white radish
    (about 1 pound)
  3 large carrots
  1 large cucumber, seeded
    (page 44)
  4 stalks celery, diagonally cut
    into $\frac{1}{2}$-inch pieces
  8 green onions, diagonally cut
    into $\frac{1}{4}$-inch pieces
  1 large red pepper, cut into
    $\frac{1}{2}$-inch pieces
  1 large green pepper, cut into
    $\frac{1}{2}$-inch pieces
  4 ounces fresh ginger, peeled and
    thinly sliced
  Green Onion Curls for garnish
    (page 22)

1. Combine all pickling liquid ingredients in 3-quart saucepan. Bring to a boil over medium heat, stirring occasionally. Cool.

2. Cut radish into matchstick pieces. Repeat with carrots and cucumber.

3. Fill large saucepan or Dutch oven $\frac{1}{2}$ full with water. Bring to a boil. Add all vegetables. Remove from heat. Let stand 2 minutes.

4. Drain vegetables in large colander. Spread vegetables out onto clean towels; allow to dry 2 to 3 hours.

5. Pack vegetables firmly into clean jars with tight-fitting lids. Pour Pickling Liquid into jars to cover vegetables. Seal jars tightly. Store in refrigerator at least 1 week before using. Serve garnished, if desired.

*Makes 1$\frac{1}{2}$ to 2 quarts*

Step 2. Cutting radish.

Step 4. Drying cooked vegetables.

Step 5. Covering vegetables with Pickling Liquid.

# Braised Lion's Head

**Meatballs**
 1 pound lean ground pork
 4 ounces shrimp, shelled, deveined
  and finely chopped
 1/4 cup sliced water chestnuts,
  finely chopped
 1 teaspoon minced fresh ginger
 1 green onion with top, finely
  chopped
 1 tablespoon soy sauce
 1 tablespoon dry sherry
 1/2 teaspoon salt
 1/2 teaspoon sugar
 1 tablespoon cornstarch
 1 egg, lightly beaten
 2 tablespoons vegetable oil

**Sauce**
 1 1/2 cups chicken broth
 2 tablespoons soy sauce
 1/2 teaspoon sugar
 1 head napa cabbage (1 1/2 to
  2 pounds)
 2 tablespoons cornstarch
 3 tablespoons cold water
 1 teaspoon sesame oil
  Green Onion Curls (page 22)
  and fresh dill for garnish

1. Combine all meatball ingredients except vegetable oil in large bowl; mix well. Divide mixture into eight portions; shape each portion into ball.

2. Heat vegetable oil in wok or large nonstick skillet over medium-high heat. Add meatballs; cook 6 to 8 minutes or until browned, stirring occasionally.

3. Transfer meatballs to large saucepan; discard drippings. Add chicken broth, soy sauce and sugar to saucepan. Bring to a boil. Reduce heat to low; cover. Simmer 30 minutes.

4. While meatballs are cooking, remove core from cabbage.

5. Cut base of cabbage leaves into 2-inch squares. Cut leafy tops in half.

6. Place cabbage over meatballs; cover. Simmer an additional 10 minutes.

7. Using slotted spoon, transfer cabbage and meatballs to serving platter. Blend cornstarch and water in small cup. Gradually add to pan juices, stirring constantly; cook until slightly thickened. Stir in sesame oil. Serve over meatballs and cabbage. Garnish, if desired.

*Makes 4 to 6 servings*

Step 4. Removing core from cabbage.

Step 6. Placing cabbage over meatballs.

# Two-Onion Pork Shreds

1/2 teaspoon Szechuan
    peppercorns*
1 teaspoon cornstarch
4 teaspoons soy sauce, divided
4 teaspoons dry sherry, divided
7 1/2 teaspoons vegetable oil, divided
8 ounces boneless lean pork
2 teaspoons red wine vinegar
1/2 teaspoon sugar
2 cloves garlic, minced
1/2 small yellow onion, cut into
    1/4-inch slices
8 green onions with tops, cut into
    2-inch pieces
1/2 teaspoon sesame oil

*Szechuan peppercorns are deceptively potent. Wear rubber or plastic gloves when crushing them and do not touch your eyes or lips when handling.

1. For marinade, place peppercorns in small skillet. Cook over medium-low heat, shaking skillet frequently, until fragrant, about 2 minutes. Let cool.

2. Crush peppercorns with mortar and pestle (or place between paper towels and crush with hammer).

3. Transfer peppercorns to medium bowl. Add cornstarch, 2 teaspoons soy sauce, 2 teaspoons sherry and 1 1/2 teaspoons vegetable oil; mix well.

4. Slice meat 1/8-inch thick; cut into 2 × 1/2-inch pieces. Add to marinade; stir to coat well. Cover and refrigerate 30 minutes, stirring occasionally.

5. Combine remaining 2 teaspoons soy sauce, 2 teaspoons sherry, vinegar and sugar in small bowl; mix well.

6. Heat remaining 6 teaspoons vegetable oil in wok or large skillet over high heat. Stir in garlic. Add meat mixture; stir-fry until no longer pink in center, about 2 minutes. Add yellow onion; stir-fry 1 minute. Add green onion; stir-fry 30 seconds.

7. Add soy-vinegar mixture; cook and stir 30 seconds. Stir in sesame oil.

*Makes 2 to 3 servings*

Step 2. Crushing peppercorns.

Step 4. Adding meat to marinade.

Step 6. Adding green onion to wok.

# Satay Beef

1 pound beef tenderloin, trimmed
1 teaspoon cornstarch
5 tablespoons water, divided
3½ teaspoons soy sauce, divided
1 to 2 teaspoons sesame oil
2 tablespoons vegetable oil
1 medium onion, coarsely
    chopped
1 clove garlic, minced
1 tablespoon dry sherry
1 tablespoon satay sauce
1 teaspoon curry powder
½ teaspoon sugar
    Fresh chervil and carrot
    flowers* for garnish

*To make carrot flower garnish, cut carrot crosswise into thin slices; cut into desired shape with small decorative cutter or sharp knife.

1. Cut meat across grain into thin slices. Flatten each slice by pressing with fingers; place in medium bowl.

2. Combine cornstarch, 3 tablespoons water, 1½ teaspoons soy sauce and sesame oil in small cup or bowl; mix well. Add to meat; stir to coat well. Let stand 20 minutes.

3. Heat vegetable oil in wok or large skillet over high heat. Add ½ of meat, spreading out slices so they do not overlap.

4. Cook meat slices on each side just until lightly browned, 2 to 3 minutes. Remove from wok; set aside. Repeat with remaining meat slices.

5. Add onion and garlic to wok; stir-fry until tender, about 3 minutes.

6. Combine remaining 2 tablespoons water, 2 teaspoons soy sauce, sherry, satay sauce, curry powder and sugar in small cup. Add to wok; cook and stir until liquid boils. Return meat to wok; cook and stir until thoroughly heated. Garnish, if desired. *Makes 4 servings*

Step 1. Flattening meat.

Step 2. Adding soy sauce mixture to meat.

Step 3. Placing meat in wok.

# Honey-Glazed Spareribs

1 side pork spareribs (about
   2 pounds)
¼ cup *plus* 1 tablespoon soy sauce,
   divided
3 tablespoons hoisin sauce
3 tablespoons dry sherry, divided
1 tablespoon sugar
1 teaspoon minced fresh ginger
2 cloves garlic, minced
¼ teaspoon Chinese five-spice
   powder
2 tablespoons honey
1 tablespoon cider vinegar
   Green Onion Curls (page 22),
   slivered green onions and
   edible flowers for garnish

1. Have your butcher cut ribs down length of slab into two pieces so that each half is 2 to 3 inches wide. Cut between bones to make 6-inch pieces.

2. Trim excess fat from ribs. Place ribs in heavy resealable plastic bag.

3. For marinade, combine ¼ cup soy sauce, hoisin sauce, 2 tablespoons sherry, sugar, ginger, garlic and five-spice powder in small cup or bowl; mix well. Pour over ribs.

4. Seal bag tightly; place in large bowl. Refrigerate at least 8 hours or overnight, turning bag occasionally.

5. Preheat oven to 350°F. Line large baking pan with foil. Place ribs on rack in pan, reserving marinade. Bake 30 minutes; turn ribs over. Brush with marinade; continue baking 40 minutes or until ribs are tender when pierced with fork.

6. For glaze, combine honey, vinegar, remaining 1 tablespoon soy sauce and 1 tablespoon sherry in small bowl; mix well. Brush ½ of mixture over ribs. Place under broiler 4 to 6 inches from heat source; broil until glaze is hot and bubbly, 2 to 3 minutes. Turn ribs over. Brush with remaining honey glaze.

7. Broil until hot and bubbly. Cut into serving-size pieces. Garnish, if desired.

*Makes about 4 servings*

Step 1. Cutting ribs into 6-inch pieces.

Step 3. Pouring marinade over ribs.

Step 6. Brushing ribs with glaze.

# *Mongolian Lamb*

**Sesame Sauce**
- 1 tablespoon sesame seeds
- 1/4 cup soy sauce
- 1 tablespoon dry sherry
- 1 tablespoon red wine vinegar
- 1 1/2 teaspoons sugar
- 1 clove garlic, minced
- 1 green onion with top, finely chopped
- 1/2 teaspoon sesame oil

**Lamb**
- 1 pound boneless lean lamb* (leg or shoulder)
- 2 small leeks
- 4 green onions with tops
- 2 medium carrots, shredded
- 1 medium zucchini, shredded
- 1 *each* green and red pepper, cut into matchstick pieces
- 1/2 small head napa cabbage, thinly sliced
- 1 cup bean sprouts
- 4 tablespoons vegetable oil, divided
- 4 slices peeled fresh ginger
- Chili oil (optional)

*Or, substitute beef flank steak or boneless lean pork for the lamb.

1. For Sesame Sauce, place sesame seeds in small skillet. Carefully shake or stir over medium heat until seeds begin to pop and turn golden brown, about 2 minutes; cool.

2. Crush seeds with mortar and pestle (or place between paper towels and crush with rolling pin); scrape up sesame paste with knife and transfer to small serving bowl. Add remaining sauce ingredients; mix well.

3. Slice meat across grain into 2 × 1/4-inch strips.

4. Cut leek into 2-inch slivers. Repeat with green onions.

5. Arrange meat and all vegetables on large platter. Have Sesame Sauce, vegetable oil, ginger and chili oil near cooking area.

6. Heat wok or electric griddle to 350°F. Cook one serving at a time. For each serving, heat 1 tablespoon vegetable oil. Add one slice ginger; cook and stir 30 seconds. Discard ginger. Add 1/2 cup meat strips; stir-fry until lightly browned, about 1 minute. Add 2 cups assorted vegetables; stir-fry 1 minute. Drizzle with 2 tablespoons Sesame Sauce; stir-fry 30 seconds. Season with a few drops chili oil. Repeat with remaining ingredients.

*Makes 4 servings*

Step 4. Cutting leek.

Step 5. Arranging cut-up ingredients on platter.

# Sweet and Sour Pork

1 egg yolk, lightly beaten
¼ cup soy sauce
1½ tablespoons dry sherry
2 teaspoons sugar
2 pounds boneless lean pork, cut into 1-inch pieces
½ cup *plus* 2 tablespoons cornstarch, divided
1 can (20 ounces) pineapple chunks in syrup, undrained
¼ cup rice vinegar
3 tablespoons tomato sauce
1 cup water
1 medium cucumber
3 cups *plus* 3 tablespoons vegetable oil, divided
1 large yellow onion, thinly sliced
8 green onions with tops, diagonally cut into 1-inch pieces
1 red or green pepper, chopped
4 ounces fresh mushrooms, cut into quarters
2 stalks celery, diagonally cut into ½-inch slices
Celery leaves and red pepper curls* for garnish

*To make red pepper curls, cut additional red pepper into thin strips. Add to small bowl of salted water. Let stand until slightly softened, 1 to 2 hours. Wrap pepper strips around finger to curl.

1. For marinade, combine egg yolk, soy sauce, sherry and sugar in large bowl. Add meat; stir to coat well. Cover and refrigerate 1 hour, stirring occasionally.

2. Drain meat, reserving marinade. Place ½ cup cornstarch in large bowl. Add meat; toss to coat well. Set aside.

3. Drain pineapple, reserving syrup. Add syrup to reserved marinade with vinegar and tomato sauce; stir until well blended. Set aside. Combine remaining 2 tablespoons cornstarch and water in another small bowl; mix well. Set aside.

4. Cut cucumber in half lengthwise; remove seeds.

5. Cut cucumber into ¼-inch pieces; set aside.

6. Heat 3 cups oil in wok or large skillet over high heat to 375°F. Add ½ of meat. Cook until no longer pink in center, about 5 minutes; drain on paper towels. Repeat with remaining meat.

7. Heat remaining 3 tablespoons oil in wok over high heat. Add vegetables; stir-fry 3 minutes. Stir cornstarch mixture. Add to wok with pineapple syrup mixture; cook and stir until sauce boils and thickens. Add meat and pineapple; stir-fry until thoroughly heated. Garnish, if desired. *Makes 4 servings*

Step 2. Coating pork with cornstarch.

Step 4. Removing cucumber seeds.

# Beef with Cashews

**1 piece fresh ginger (about 1 inch square)**
**1 pound beef rump steak**
**4 tablespoons vegetable oil, divided**
**4 teaspoons cornstarch**
**½ cup water**
**4 teaspoons soy sauce**
**1 teaspoon sesame oil**
**1 teaspoon oyster sauce**
**1 teaspoon Chinese chili sauce**
**8 green onions with tops, cut into 1-inch pieces**
**2 cloves garlic, minced**
**⅔ cup unsalted roasted cashews (about 3 ounces)**
**Fresh carrot slices and thyme leaves for garnish**

1. Peel and finely chop ginger; set aside.

2. Trim fat from meat; discard. Cut meat across grain into thin slices, each about 2 inches long.

3. Heat 1 tablespoon vegetable oil in wok or large skillet over high heat. Add ½ of meat; stir-fry until browned, 3 to 5 minutes. Remove from wok; set aside. Repeat with 1 tablespoon oil and remaining meat.

4. Combine cornstarch, water, soy sauce, sesame oil, oyster sauce and chili sauce in small bowl; mix well.

5. Heat remaining 2 tablespoons vegetable oil in wok or large skillet over high heat. Add ginger, onions, garlic and cashews; stir-fry 1 minute.

6. Stir cornstarch mixture; add to wok with meat. Cook and stir until liquid boils and thickens. Garnish, if desired.

*Makes 4 servings*

Step 1. Chopping peeled ginger.

Step 2. Cutting meat.

Step 5. Adding cashews to wok.

# Beef with Peppers

1 ounce dried mushrooms
    Water
1 teaspoon cornstarch
1 teaspoon instant beef bouillon
    granules
1 tablespoon soy sauce
1 teaspoon sesame oil
1 pound beef tenderloin, trimmed
2½ tablespoons vegetable oil
1 clove garlic, minced
¼ teaspoon Chinese five-spice
    powder
2 small onions, cut into wedges
1 green pepper, thinly sliced
1 green pepper, thinly sliced
1 red pepper, thinly sliced
8 ounces Chinese-style thin egg
    noodles, cooked and drained
    (optional)

1. Place mushrooms in medium bowl; add enough warm water to cover mushrooms completely. Let stand 30 minutes; drain.

2. Squeeze excess water from mushrooms. Remove and discard stems. Slice caps into thin strips.

3. Combine cornstarch, bouillon granules, additional ¼ cup water, soy sauce and sesame oil in small bowl; mix well. Set aside.

4. Cut meat into thin slices, each about 1 inch long.

5. Heat vegetable oil in wok or large skillet over high heat. Add garlic and five-spice powder; stir-fry 15 seconds.

6. Add meat to wok; stir-fry until browned, about 5 minutes. Add onions; stir-fry 2 minutes. Add mushrooms and peppers; stir-fry until peppers are crisp-tender, about 2 minutes.

7. Stir cornstarch mixture; add to wok. Cook and stir until liquid boils and thickens. Serve over hot cooked noodles.

*Makes 4 servings*

Step 2. Removing stems from mushrooms.

Step 4. Slicing meat.

Step 6. Adding mushrooms and peppers to wok.

# Vermicelli with Pork

4 ounces Chinese rice vermicelli
  *or* bean threads
32 dried mushrooms
 1 small red *or* green hot chili
   pepper*
 3 green onions with tops, divided
 2 tablespoons minced fresh ginger
 2 tablespoons hot bean sauce
1½ cups chicken broth
 1 tablespoon soy sauce
 1 tablespoon dry sherry
 2 tablespoons vegetable oil
 6 ounces lean ground pork
   Fresh cilantro leaves and hot
   red pepper for garnish
   Cilantro leaves and fresh hot
   red pepper for garnish

*Hot chili peppers are deceptively potent.
Wear rubber or plastic gloves when
removing seeds or chopping peppers and
do not touch your eyes or lips when
handling.

1. Place vermicelli and dried mushrooms in separate large bowls; cover each with hot water. Let stand 30 minutes; drain. Cut vermicelli into 4- inch pieces.

2. Squeeze out as much excess water as possible from mushrooms. Cut off and discard mushroom stems; cut caps into thin slices.

3. Cut chili pepper in half; scrape out seeds.

4. Finely chop chili pepper.

5. Cut one onion into 1½-inch slivers; reserve for garnish. Cut remaining two onions into thin slices.

6. Combine ginger and hot bean sauce in small bowl; set aside. Combine chicken broth, soy sauce and sherry in another small bowl; set aside.

7. Heat oil in wok or large skillet over high heat. Add meat; stir-fry until no longer pink, about 2 minutes. Add chili pepper, sliced onions and bean sauce mixture; stir-fry 1 minute.

8. Add chicken broth mixture, vermicelli and mushrooms. Simmer, uncovered, until most of the liquid is absorbed, about 5 minutes. Top with onion slivers. Garnish, if desired.

*Makes 4 servings*

Step 1. Cutting vermicelli.

Step 2. Slicing mushrooms.

Step 3. Removing pepper seeds.

# Mu Shu Pork

4 teaspoons cornstarch, divided
8 teaspoons soy sauce, divided
5 teaspoons dry sherry, divided
8 ounces boneless lean pork, cut
    into matchstick pieces
3 dried mushrooms
2 dried wood ears
    Water
1/2 teaspoon sugar
1 teaspoon sesame oil
2 tablespoons *plus* 1 teaspoon
    vegetable oil, divided
2 eggs, lightly beaten
1 teaspoon minced fresh ginger
1/2 cup sliced bamboo shoots
    (1/2 of 8-ounce can), cut into
    matchstick pieces
1 small carrot, shredded
1/2 cup chicken broth
2 cups bean sprouts (about
    4 ounces)
2 green onions with tops, cut into
    1 1/2-inch slivers
1/2 cup hoisin sauce
16 Mandarin Pancakes (recipe
    follows on page 54)

1. For marinade, combine 1 teaspoon cornstarch, 2 teaspoons soy sauce and 2 teaspoons sherry in large bowl. Add meat; stir to coat. Let stand 30 minutes.

2. Meanwhile, place dried mushrooms and wood ears in small bowl; add enough water to cover. Let stand 30 minutes; drain. Squeeze out excess water. Cut off and discard mushroom stems; cut caps into thin slices.

3. Pinch out hard nobs from center of wood ears; discard.

4. Cut wood ears into thin strips.

5. Combine remaining 3 teaspoons cornstarch, 6 teaspoons soy sauce and 3 teaspoons sherry in small bowl. Add additional 1 tablespoon water, sugar and sesame oil; mix well.

6. Heat 1/2 teaspoon vegetable oil in small nonstick skillet over medium-high heat. Add 1/2 of eggs, tilting skillet to cover bottom.

7. Cook eggs just until set. Loosen edges and turn omelet over; cook 5 seconds.

8. Remove omelet from skillet; set aside to cool. Repeat with another 1/2 teaspoon vegetable oil and remaining eggs.

9. Cut omelets in half. Stack halves; cut crosswise into thin strips.

10. Heat remaining 2 tablespoons vegetable oil in wok or large skillet over high heat. Stir in ginger. Add meat; stir-fry until meat is no longer pink in center, about 2 minutes. Add mushrooms, wood ears, bamboo shoots, carrot and chicken broth; stir-fry 2 minutes.

Step 3. Removing nobs from wood ears.

Step 6. Tilting skillet to cover bottom with eggs.

Step 7. Loosening omelet from skillet.

*continued on page 54*

**Mu Shu Pork, continued**

11. Add bean sprouts and onions; stir-fry 1 minute.

12. Stir cornstarch mixture; add to wok. Cook, stirring constantly, until sauce bubbles and thickens. Stir in omelet strips.

13. To serve, spread about 2 teaspoons hoisin sauce onto each pancake. Spoon about 3 tablespoons pork mixture down center. Fold over bottom; roll up.

*Makes 8 servings*

# Mandarin Pancakes

**2 cups all-purpose flour**
**³/4 cup boiling water**
**2 tablespoons sesame oil**

1. Place flour in bowl; make well in center. Pour in boiling water.

2. Stir flour mixture with wooden spoon until dough looks like lumpy meal.

3. Press dough into ball. On lightly floured surface, knead dough until smooth and satiny, about 5 minutes (page 12). Cover with clean towel and let rest 30 minutes.

4. Roll dough into log, 10 inches long. Cut into 1-inch pieces; cover with plastic wrap.

5. Cut each piece of dough in half, keeping remaining dough pieces covered with plastic wrap. Shape each half into ball. Place on lightly floured surface; flatten slightly. With lightly floured rolling pin, roll each dough piece into 3-inch circle; brush with small amount of sesame oil. Stack two dough circles together, oil-side in.

6. Roll each pair of dough circles into 6- to 7-inch circle; cover and set aside. Repeat with remaining dough circles.

7. Heat nonstick skillet over medium-low heat. Cook pancakes, one pair at a time, turning every 30 seconds, until cakes are flecked with brown and feel dry, 2 to 3 minutes. (Be careful not to overcook pancakes or they will become brittle.)

8. Remove pancakes from pan. Separate each pancake into two pancakes while still hot. Stack pancakes on plate; keep covered while cooking remaining pancakes. Fold pancakes into quarters and arrange in serving basket. Serve immediately.

*Makes about 20 pancakes*

**Note:** Pancakes may be prepared ahead and refrigerated or frozen in resealable plastic bags.

To reheat, wrap pancakes in clean towel (thaw completely, if using frozen). Steam over simmering water 5 minutes.

Mandarin Pancakes: Step 2. Stirring flour mixture to form dough.

Mandarin Pancakes: Step 6. Rolling out dough circles.

Mandarin Pancakes: Step 7. Cooking pancakes.

# How to Cut Chicken Chinese-Style

Recipes for Chinese chicken dishes often instruct that chicken be cut into serving-size pieces. These pieces should be smaller than chicken pieces generally are cut. Following are directions for cutting a whole chicken Chinese-style. A cleaver is the best utensil for chopping a chicken, although poultry shears or a sharp knife may also be used.

1. Place chicken, breast-side up, on heavy cutting board. Cut in half lengthwise, cutting slightly to one side of breastbone and backbone. (Cut completely through chicken to make two pieces.)

2. Remove and discard backbone, if desired.

3. Pull each leg up slightly from breast section; cut through ball and socket joint to remove each leg. Cut through knee joint of each leg to separate into drumstick and thigh.

4. Pull each wing away from breast; cut through joint next to breast.

5. Cut each drumstick, thigh and breast piece crosswise into three pieces, cutting completely through bones. Cut each wing into two pieces.

*Makes 22 small serving-size pieces*

Step 1. Cutting chicken in half.

Step 3. Cutting knee joint.

Step 4. Cutting wing joint.

# Hoisin Chicken

1 broiler-fryer chicken (3 to
    4 pounds)
1/2 cup *plus* 1 tablespoon
    cornstarch, divided
1 cup water
3 tablespoons dry sherry
3 tablespoons cider vinegar
3 tablespoons hoisin sauce
4 teaspoons soy sauce
2 teaspoons instant chicken
    bouillon granules
    Vegetable oil for frying
2 teaspoons minced fresh ginger
2 medium onions, chopped
8 ounces fresh broccoli, cut into
    1-inch pieces
1 red or green pepper, chopped
2 cans (4 ounces *each*) whole
    button mushrooms, drained
    Vermicelli (page 93), optional
    Additional red pepper, cut into
    matchstick pieces, for garnish

1. Rinse chicken; cut Chinese-style (page 55).

2. Combine 1 tablespoon cornstarch, water, sherry, vinegar, hoisin sauce, soy sauce and bouillon granules in small bowl; mix well. Set aside.

3. Place remaining 1/2 cup cornstarch in large bowl. Add chicken pieces; stir to coat well.

4. Heat oil in large skillet or wok over high heat to 375°F. Add 1/3 of the chicken pieces, one at a time; cook until no longer pink in center, about 5 minutes. Drain chicken pieces on paper towels. Repeat with remaining chicken.

5. Remove all but 2 tablespoons oil from skillet. Add ginger to skillet; stir-fry 1 minute. Add onions; stir-fry 1 minute. Add broccoli, red pepper and mushrooms; stir-fry 2 minutes.

6. Stir cornstarch mixture; add to skillet. Cook and stir until sauce boils and thickens.

7. Return chicken to skillet. Cook and stir until chicken is thoroughly heated, about 2 minutes. Serve over hot Vermicelli and garnish, if desired. *Makes 6 servings*

Step 1. Cutting chicken Chinese-style.

Step 4. Cooking chicken.

# Kung Pao Chicken

3½ teaspoons cornstarch, divided
5 teaspoons soy sauce, divided
5 teaspoons dry sherry, divided
¼ teaspoon salt
3 boneless skinless chicken breast halves, cut into bite-size pieces
1 tablespoon red wine vinegar
2 tablespoons chicken broth *or* water
1½ teaspoons sugar
3 tablespoons vegetable oil, divided
⅓ cup salted peanuts
6 to 8 small dried hot chili peppers
1½ teaspoons minced fresh ginger
2 green onions with tops, cut into 1½-inch pieces
Additional green onion and dried hot chili pepper for garnish

1. For marinade, combine 2 teaspoons cornstarch, 2 teaspoons soy sauce, 2 teaspoons sherry and salt in large bowl; mix well. Add chicken; stir to coat well. Let stand 30 minutes.

2. Combine remaining 1½ teaspoons cornstarch, 3 teaspoons soy sauce, 3 teaspoons sherry, vinegar, chicken broth and sugar in small bowl; mix well. Set aside.

3. Heat 1 tablespoon oil in wok or large skillet over medium heat. Add peanuts; cook and stir until lightly toasted. Remove peanuts from wok; set aside.

4. Heat remaining 2 tablespoons oil in wok over medium heat. Add chili peppers; stir-fry until peppers just begin to char, about 1 minute.

5. Increase heat to high. Add chicken mixture; stir-fry 2 minutes. Add ginger; stir-fry until chicken is no longer pink in center, about 1 minute.

6. Add peanuts and onions; stir-fry 1 minute.

7. Stir cornstarch mixture; add to wok. Cook and stir until sauce boils and thickens. Garnish, if desired.                *Makes 3 servings*

Step 3. Toasting peanuts.

Step 4. Stir-frying chili peppers.

Step 6. Stir-frying peanuts and onions with chicken mixture.

# Lemon Chicken

4 whole boneless skinless chicken
    breasts
$\frac{1}{2}$ cup cornstarch
$\frac{1}{2}$ teaspoon salt
$\frac{1}{8}$ teaspoon pepper
4 egg yolks, lightly beaten
$\frac{1}{4}$ cup water
    Vegetable oil for frying
4 green onions with tops, sliced

**Lemon Sauce**
3 tablespoons cornstarch
$1\frac{1}{2}$ cups water
$\frac{1}{2}$ cup lemon juice
$3\frac{1}{2}$ tablespoons packed brown
    sugar
3 tablespoons honey
2 teaspoons instant chicken
    bouillon granules
1 teaspoon minced fresh ginger

    Lemon peel and lemon balm for
    garnish

1. Cut chicken breasts in half; place between two sheets of plastic wrap. Pound with mallet or rolling pin to flatten slightly.

2. Combine cornstarch, salt and pepper in small bowl. Gradually blend in egg yolks and water.

3. Heat oil in wok or large skillet over high heat to 375°F. Meanwhile, dip chicken breasts, one at a time, into batter.

4. Add chicken breasts, two at a time, to hot oil; cook until golden brown, about 5 minutes. Drain chicken on paper towels. Keep warm while cooking remaining chicken.

5. Cut each breast into four pieces. Arrange chicken pieces on serving plate. Sprinkle with onions. Keep warm.

6. Combine cornstarch, water, lemon juice, brown sugar, honey, boullion granules and ginger in medium saucepan; mix well. Cook over medium heat, stirring constantly, until sauce boils and thickens, about 5 minutes. Pour over chicken. Garnish, if desired.

*Makes 4 to 6 servings*

Step 1. Pounding chicken breasts to flatten.

Step 3. Dipping chicken into batter.

Step 4. Cooking chicken.

# Chicken Chow Mein

Fried Noodles (page 92)
2 whole chicken breasts
8 ounces boneless lean pork
3 teaspoons cornstarch, divided
2$\frac{1}{2}$ tablespoons dry sherry, divided
2 tablespoons soy sauce, divided
$\frac{1}{2}$ cup water
2 teaspoons instant chicken
    bouillon granules
2 tablespoons vegetable oil
1 piece fresh ginger (1-inch
    square), peeled and finely
    chopped
1 clove garlic, minced
8 ounces deveined shelled shrimp
    (page 74)
2 medium yellow onions, chopped
1 red or green pepper, thinly
    sliced
2 stalks celery, diagonally cut
    into 1-inch slices
8 green onions with tops, chopped
4 ounces cabbage ($\frac{1}{4}$ of small
    head), shredded

1. Prepare Fried Noodles; set aside.

2. Remove skin and bones from chicken breasts.

3. Cut chicken and pork into 1-inch pieces.

4. Combine 1 teaspoon cornstarch, 1$\frac{1}{2}$ teaspoons sherry and 1$\frac{1}{2}$ teaspoons soy sauce in large bowl. Add chicken and pork; toss to coat well. Cover and refrigerate 1 hour.

5. Combine remaining 2 teaspoons cornstarch, 2 tablespoons sherry, 1$\frac{1}{2}$ tablespoons soy sauce, water and boullion granules in small bowl; set aside.

6. Heat oil in wok or large skillet over high heat. Add ginger and garlic; stir-fry 1 minute. Add chicken and pork; stir-fry until no longer pink in center, about 5 minutes. Add shrimp; stir-fry until shrimp turn pink, about 3 minutes.

7. Add vegetables to wok; stir-fry until crisp-tender, 3 to 5 minutes. Add bouillon-soy sauce mixture. Cook and stir until sauce boils and thickens; cook and stir an additional minute.

8. Arrange Fried Noodles on serving plate; top with chicken mixture.

*Makes 6 servings*

Step 2. Removing chicken bones.

Step 3. Cutting chicken and pork.

Step 6. Stir-frying shrimp with chicken mixture.

# Asparagus Chicken with Black Bean Sauce

5 teaspoons cornstarch, divided
4 teaspoons soy sauce, divided
1 tablespoon dry sherry
1 teaspoon sesame oil
3 boneless skinless chicken breast halves, cut into bite-size pieces
1 tablespoon fermented, salted black beans
1 teaspoon minced fresh ginger
1 clove garlic, minced
$\frac{1}{2}$ cup chicken broth
1 tablespoon oyster sauce
1 medium yellow onion
3 tablespoons vegetable oil, divided
1 pound fresh asparagus spears, trimmed and diagonally cut into 1-inch pieces
2 tablespoons water
Fresh cilantro leaves for garnish

1. Combine 2 teaspoons cornstarch, 2 teaspoons soy sauce, sherry and sesame oil in large bowl; mix well. Add chicken; stir to coat well. Let stand 30 minutes.

2. Place beans in sieve; rinse under cold running water. Finely chop beans. Combine with ginger and garlic; set aside.

3. Combine remaining 3 teaspoons cornstarch, remaining 2 teaspoons soy sauce, chicken broth and oyster sauce in small bowl; mix well. Set aside.

4. Peel onion; cut into eight wedges. Separate wedges; set aside.

5. Heat 2 tablespoons vegetable oil in wok or large skillet over high heat. Add chicken mixture; stir-fry until chicken is no longer pink in center, about 3 minutes. Remove from wok; set aside.

6. Heat remaining 1 tablespoon vegetable oil in wok. Add onion and asparagus; stir-fry 30 seconds.

7. Add water; cover. Cook, stirring occasionally, until asparagus is crisp-tender, about 2 minutes. Return chicken to wok.

8. Stir chicken broth mixture; add to wok with bean mixture. Cook until sauce boils and thickens, stirring constantly. Garnish, if desired.

*Makes 3 to 4 servings*

Step 4. Separating onion wedges.

Step 6. Stir-frying onion and asparagus.

# Chicken with Lychees

**3 whole boneless skinless chicken breasts**
**¼ cup *plus* 1 teaspoon cornstarch, divided**
**½ cup water, divided**
**½ cup tomato sauce**
**1 teaspoon sugar**
**1 teaspoon instant chicken bouillon granules**
**3 tablespoons vegetable oil**
**1 red pepper, cut into 1-inch pieces**
**6 green onions with tops, cut into 1-inch pieces**
**1 can (11 ounces) whole peeled lychees, drained**
**Vermicelli (page 93), optional**
**Fresh cilantro leaves for garnish**

1. Cut chicken breasts in half; cut each half into six pieces.

2. Place ¼ cup cornstarch in large resealable plastic bag. Add chicken pieces; close bag tightly. Shake bag until chicken is well coated; set aside.

3. Combine remaining 1 teaspoon cornstarch and ¼ cup water in small bowl; mix well. Set aside.

4. Combine remaining ¼ cup water, tomato sauce, sugar and bouillon granules in small bowl; mix well. Set aside.

5. Heat oil in wok or large skillet over high heat. Add chicken; stir-fry until lightly browned, 5 to 8 minutes. Add red pepper and onions; stir-fry 1 minute.

6. Pour tomato sauce mixture over chicken mixture. Stir in lychees.

7. Reduce heat to low; cover. Simmer until chicken is tender and no longer pink in center, about 5 minutes.

8. Stir cornstarch mixture; add to wok. Cook and stir until sauce boils and thickens. Serve over hot Vermicelli and garnish, if desired.

*Makes 4 servings*

Step 1. Cutting chicken.

Step 2. Coating chicken with cornstarch.

Step 6. Stirring lychees into other ingredients in wok.

# *Almond Chicken*

2½ tablespoons cornstarch, divided
1½ cups water
  4 tablespoons dry sherry, divided
  4 teaspoons soy sauce
  1 teaspoon instant chicken
    bouillon granules
  1 egg white
½ teaspoon salt
  4 whole boneless skinless chicken
    breasts, cut into 1-inch pieces
    Vegetable oil for frying
½ cup blanched whole almonds
    (about 3 ounces)
  1 large carrot, finely chopped
  1 teaspoon minced fresh ginger
  6 green onions with tops, cut into
    1-inch pieces
  3 stalks celery, diagonally cut
    into ½-inch pieces
  8 fresh mushrooms, sliced
½ cup sliced bamboo shoots (½ of
    8-ounce can), drained
    Fried Noodles (page 92),
    optional
    Carrot strips and fresh cilantro
    leaves for garnish

1. Combine 1½ tablespoons cornstarch, water, 2 tablespoons sherry, soy sauce and bouillon granules in small saucepan. Cook and stir over medium heat until mixture boils and thickens, about 5 minutes; keep warm.

2. Beat egg white in medium bowl until foamy.

3. Add remaining 1 tablespoon cornstarch, 2 tablespoons sherry and salt to egg white; mix well. Add chicken pieces; stir to coat well.

4. Heat oil in wok or large skillet over high heat to 375°F. Add ⅓ of chicken pieces, one at a time; cook until no longer pink in center, 3 to 5 minutes. Drain chicken pieces on paper towels. Repeat with remaining chicken.

5. Remove all but 2 tablespoons oil from wok. Add almonds; stir-fry until golden brown, about 2 minutes. Remove almonds from wok; set aside.

6. Add carrot and ginger to wok; stir-fry 1 minute. Add onions, celery, mushrooms and bamboo shoots; stir-fry until crisp-tender, about 3 minutes. Stir in chicken, almonds and cornstarch mixture; cook and stir until thoroughly heated. Serve with Fried Noodles and garnish, if desired.

*Makes 4 to 6 servings*

Step 1. Cooking sauce.

Step 2. Beating egg white.

Step 4. Cooking chicken.

# Chinese Chicken Salad

2 whole chicken breasts
4 cups water
1 tablespoon dry sherry
2 slices peeled fresh ginger
5 green onions with tops, divided
¼ cup Chinese plum sauce
2 tablespoons rice vinegar
1 tablespoon vegetable oil
1 tablespoon sesame oil
1½ teaspoons soy sauce
4½ teaspoons sugar
1 teaspoon dry mustard
3 tablespoons slivered almonds
2 tablespoons sesame seeds
4 cups shredded iceberg lettuce
1 small carrot, shredded
1½ cups bean sprouts (about
    3 ounces)
¼ cup fresh cilantro leaves
    (Chinese parsley)
    Bean threads *or* Vermicelli
    (page 93), cooked and drained
    Additional fresh cilantro leaves
    and edible flowers for garnish

1. Combine chicken, water, sherry, ginger and two whole green onions in 3-quart saucepan. Bring to a boil over medium-high heat. Reduce heat to low; cover. Simmer 20 minutes or until chicken is no longer pink in center.

2. Remove saucepan from heat. Let stand until chicken is cool. Remove chicken from stock; set aside. Strain stock; refrigerate or freeze for another use.

3. Remove and discard skin and bones from chicken. Pull meat into long shreds; set aside

4. For dressing, combine plum sauce, vinegar, vegetable and sesame oils, soy sauce, sugar and mustard in small bowl; mix well. Set aside.

5. Toast almonds by shaking in small dry skillet over medium heat until golden brown and fragrant, about 3 minutes. Place in large salad bowl. Toast sesame seeds in same skillet until seeds are golden brown and begin to pop, about 2 minutes. Add sesame seeds to almonds.

6. Cut remaining three green onions with tops into 1½-inch slivers.

7. Add onions to salad bowl with lettuce, carrot, bean sprouts, cilantro, chicken and dressing; toss to coat. Add bean threads; mix lightly. Garnish, if desired.

*Makes 6 to 8 servings*

Step 1. Cooking chicken.

Step 3. Shredding chicken.

Step 6. Cutting onions into slivers.

# Combination Chop Suey

2 whole chicken breasts
4 cups chicken broth
1/2 head bok choy *or* napa cabbage
   (about 8 ounces)
2 teaspoons cornstarch
1 cup water
4 teaspoons soy sauce
1 teaspoon instant chicken
   bouillon granules
3 tablespoons vegetable oil
8 ounces boneless lean pork,
   finely chopped
4 ounces fresh green beans,
   trimmed and cut into 1-inch
   pieces
3 celery stalks, diagonally cut
   into 1/2-inch pieces
2 onions, chopped
1 large carrot, chopped
8 ounces medium shrimp, shelled
   and deveined (page 74)
1 can (8 ounces) sliced bamboo
   shoots, drained
   Steamed Rice (page 92),
   optional
   Carrot curls* and fresh thyme
   leaves for garnish

*To make carrot curls, cut thin lengthwise slice from whole peeled carrot with vegetable peeler. Roll up slice tightly, starting at short end; secure with wooden pick. Add to bowl of ice water; let stand several hours or overnight. Remove wooden picks.

1. Combine chicken and broth in large saucepan. Bring to a boil over medium-high heat. Reduce heat to low; cover. Simmer 20 to 30 minutes or until chicken is no longer pink in center. Remove from heat. Let stand until chicken is cool.

2. Remove chicken from broth; set aside. Strain broth; refrigerate or freeze for another use. Remove and discard skin and bones from chicken; coarsely chop chicken.

3. Finely chop cabbage with large knife or cleaver.

4. Combine cornstarch, water, soy sauce and bouillon granules in small bowl; set aside.

5. Heat oil in wok or large skillet over high heat. Add pork; stir-fry until no longer pink in center, about 5 minutes. Remove from wok; set aside.

6. Add cabbage, beans, celery, onions and carrot to wok; stir-fry until crisp-tender, about 3 minutes. Stir soy sauce mixture; add to wok. Cook and stir until sauce boils and thickens, about 3 minutes. Add chicken, pork, shrimp and bamboo shoots. Cook and stir until shrimp turn pink and are cooked through, about 3 minutes. Serve over hot Steamed Rice and garnish, if desired.

*Makes 4 to 6 servings*

Step 2. Removing chicken bones.

Step 3. Chopping cabbage.

# Braised Shrimp with Vegetables

1 teaspoon cornstarch
½ cup chicken broth
1 teaspoon oyster sauce
½ teaspoon minced fresh ginger
¼ teaspoon sugar
⅛ teaspoon pepper
8 ounces fresh broccoli
1 pound large shrimp
1 tablespoon vegetable oil
2 cans (4 ounces *each*) whole
   button mushrooms, drained
1 can (8 ounces) sliced bamboo
   shoots, drained

1. Combine cornstarch, broth, oyster sauce, ginger, sugar and pepper in small bowl; mix well. Set aside.

2. Remove woody stems from broccoli; discard.

3. Coarsely chop head of broccoli and remaining stems; set aside.

4. Peel shells from shrimp. Remove veins with sharp knife.

5. Heat oil in wok or large skillet over high heat. Add shrimp; stir-fry until shrimp turn pink, about 3 minutes.

6. Add broccoli to wok; stir-fry 1 minute. Add mushrooms and bamboo shoots; stir-fry 1 minute.

7. Stir cornstarch mixture; add to wok. Cook and stir until sauce boils and thickens, about 2 minutes. *Makes 4 servings*

Step 2. Removing broccoli stems.

Step 4. Deveining shrimp.

Step 5. Stir-frying shrimp.

# Scallops with Vegetables

1 ounce dried mushrooms
    Water
4 teaspoons cornstarch
2½ tablespoons dry sherry
4 teaspoons soy sauce
2 teaspoons instant chicken
    bouillon granules
8 ounces fresh green beans
1 pound fresh *or* thawed frozen
    sea scallops
2 tablespoons vegetable oil
2 yellow onions, cut into 8 wedges
    and separated (page 64)
3 stalks celery, diagonally cut
    into ½-inch pieces
2 teaspoons minced fresh ginger
1 clove garlic, minced
6 green onions with tops,
    diagonally cut into thin slices
1 can (15 ounces) baby corn,
    drained
    Whole dried mushroom and
    celery leaves for garnish

1. Place mushrooms in bowl. Add enough water to cover; let stand 30 minutes. Drain. Squeeze out as much water as possible from mushrooms. Cut off and discard stems; cut caps into thin slices.

2. Combine cornstarch and additional 1 cup water in small bowl; stir in sherry, soy sauce and bouillon granules. Set aside.

3. Trim green beans; discard ends. Diagonally cut beans into 1-inch pieces.

4. Cut scallops into quarters; set aside.

5. Heat oil in wok or large skillet over high heat. Add green beans, yellow onions, celery, ginger and garlic; stir-fry 3 minutes.

6. Stir cornstarch mixture; add to wok. Cook and stir until sauce boils and thickens.

7. Add mushrooms, scallops, green onions and baby corn.

8. Cook and stir until scallops turn opaque, about 4 minutes. Garnish, if desired.

*Makes 4 to 6 servings*

Step 3. Trimming beans.

Step 4. Quartering scallops.

Step 7. Adding corn to wok.

# Lo Mein Noodles with Shrimp

12 ounces Chinese-style thin egg noodles

2 teaspoons sesame oil
Chinese chives*

1½ tablespoons oyster sauce

1½ tablespoons soy sauce

½ teaspoon sugar

¼ teaspoon salt

¼ teaspoon ground white *or* black pepper

2 tablespoons vegetable oil

1 teaspoon minced fresh ginger

1 clove garlic, minced

8 ounces medium shrimp, shelled and deveined (page 74)

1 tablespoon dry sherry

8 ounces bean sprouts

*Or, substitute ¼ cup domestic chives cut into 1-inch pieces and 2 green onions with tops, cut into 1-inch pieces, for the Chinese chives

1. Add noodles to boiling water; cook according to package directions until tender but still firm, 2 to 3 minutes.

2. Drain noodles; rinse under cold running water. Drain again.

3. Combine noodles and sesame oil in large bowl; toss lightly to coat.

4. Cut enough chives into 1-inch pieces to measure ½ cup; set aside.

5. Combine oyster sauce, soy sauce, sugar, salt and pepper in small bowl.

6. Heat vegetable oil in wok or large skillet over high heat. Add ginger and garlic; stir-fry 10 seconds. Add shrimp; stir-fry until shrimp begin to turn pink, about 1 minute. Add chives and sherry; stir-fry until chives begin to wilt, about 15 seconds. Add ½ of the bean sprouts; stir-fry 15 seconds. Add remaining bean sprouts; stir-fry 15 seconds.

7. Add oyster sauce mixture and noodles. Cook and stir until thoroughly heated, about 2 minutes.           *Makes 4 servings*

Step 1. Adding noodles to boiling water.

Step 2. Rinsing cooked noodles.

Step 4. Snipping chives.

# Fish Rolls with Crab Sauce

1 pound sole fillets, $^1/_4$- to $^3/_8$-inch thick (about 4 ounces *each*)
1 tablespoon dry sherry
2 teaspoons sesame oil
1 green onion with top, finely chopped
1 teaspoon minced fresh ginger
$^1/_2$ teaspoon salt
Dash of ground white pepper

Crab Sauce
1$^1/_2$ tablespoons cornstarch
2 tablespoons water
1 tablespoon vegetable oil
1 teaspoon minced fresh ginger
2 green onions with tops, thinly sliced
1 tablespoon dry sherry
6 ounces fresh crabmeat, flaked
1$^1/_4$ cups chicken broth
$^1/_4$ cup milk

Scored cucumber slices,* lemon wedges and fresh tarragon leaves for garnish

*To score cucumber, run tines of fork lengthwise down all sides of cucumber before slicing.

1. If fillets are large, cut in half crosswise (each piece should be 5 to 6 inches long).

2. Combine sherry, sesame oil, chopped green onion, 1 teaspoon ginger, salt and white pepper in small bowl. Brush each piece of fish with sherry mixture; let stand 30 minutes.

3. Fold fish into thirds; place in rimmed heatproof dish that will fit inside a steamer.

4. Place dish on rack in steamer; cover steamer. Steam over boiling water until fish turns opaque and flakes easily with fork, 8 to 10 minutes. Meanwhile, combine cornstarch and water in small cup.

5. Heat vegetable oil in 2-quart saucepan over medium heat. Add 1 teaspoon ginger; cook and stir 10 seconds. Add sliced green onions, sherry and crabmeat; stir-fry 1 minute. Add chicken broth and milk; bring to a boil. Stir cornstarch mixture; add to saucepan. Cook, stirring constantly, until sauce boils and thickens slightly.

6. Using slotted spoon, transfer fish to serving platter; top with Crab Sauce. Garnish, if desired.

*Makes 4 to 6 servings*

Step 1. Brushing fish with sherry mixture.

Step 3. Placing fish in rimmed dish.

Step 4. Placing fish on rack in steamer.

# Shrimp Omelets

3 to 5 tablespoons vegetable oil, divided
8 fresh medium mushrooms, finely chopped
4 teaspoons cornstarch
1 cup water
2 teaspoons soy sauce
2 teaspoons instant chicken bouillon granules
1 teaspoon sugar
8 eggs
1/2 teaspoon salt
1/8 teaspoon pepper
8 ounces bean sprouts
8 ounces shrimp, shelled, deveined and finely chopped
4 green onions with tops, finely chopped
1 stalk celery, finely chopped
Cooked whole shrimp and slivered green onions for garnish

1. Heat 1 tablespoon oil in small skillet. Add mushrooms; cook and stir 1 minute. Remove from skillet; set aside.

2. Combine cornstarch, water, soy sauce, bouillon granules and sugar in small saucepan. Cook and stir over medium heat until mixture boils and thickens, about 5 minutes. Keep warm.

3. Combine eggs, salt and pepper in large bowl. Beat until frothy.

4. Add mushrooms, sprouts, shrimp, chopped onions and celery; mix well.

5. For each omelet, heat 1/2 tablespoon oil in 7-inch omelet pan or skillet. Pour 1/2 cup egg mixture into pan. Cook until lightly browned, 2 to 3 minutes on each side, gently pushing cooked portion to center and tilting skillet to allow uncooked portion to flow underneath.

6. Stack omelets on serving plate. Pour warm soy sauce mixture over omelets. Garnish, if desired.

*Makes 4 servings*

Step 2. Cooking sauce.

Step 3. Beating egg mixture.

Step 5. Cooking omelet.

# Seafood Combination

Fried Noodles (page 92)
8 ounces fresh *or* thawed frozen
    shrimp
8 ounces fresh *or* thawed frozen
    fish fillets
2 teaspoons cornstarch
$\frac{1}{2}$ cup water
1 tablespoon soy sauce
2 teaspoons dry sherry
1 teaspoon instant chicken
    bouillon granules
8 green onions with tops
4 tablespoons vegetable oil,
    divided
3 stalks celery, diagonally cut
    into thin slices
1 can (8 ounces) water chestnuts,
    drained and cut into halves
1 can (8 ounces) sliced bamboo
    shoots, drained
8 ounces fresh *or* thawed frozen
    sea scallops, cut into quarters

1. Prepare Fried Noodles; set aside.

2. Peel shells from shrimp; discard shells. Remove veins from shrimp (page 74); set shrimp aside.

3. Remove skin from fish fillets; discard skin.

4. Cut fillets into 1½-inch pieces; set aside.

5. Combine cornstarch, water, soy sauce, sherry and bouillon granules in small bowl; mix well. Set aside.

6. Diagonally cut green onions into thin slices.

7. Heat 2 tablespoons oil in wok or large skillet over high heat. Add green onions, celery, water chestnuts and bamboo shoots; stir-fry until crisp-tender, about 2 minutes. Remove from wok; set aside.

8. Heat remaining 2 tablespoons oil in wok over high heat. Add shrimp, fish pieces and scallops; stir-fry until all fish turns opaque and is cooked through, about 3 minutes.

9. Stir cornstarch mixture; add to wok. Cook and stir until sauce boils and thickens. Return vegetables to wok; cook and stir 2 minutes. Serve over Fried Noodles. *Makes 6 servings*

Step 2. Peeling shrimp.

Step 3. Removing skin from fish.

Step 6. Cutting onions.

# Crab-Stuffed Shrimp

## Sauce

2 tablespoons vegetable oil
1 small yellow onion, finely chopped
1 teaspoon curry powder
1½ tablespoons dry sherry
1 tablespoon satay sauce
2 teaspoons soy sauce
1 teaspoon sugar
¼ cup cream *or* milk

## Shrimp

2 egg whites, lightly beaten
4 teaspoons cornstarch
1 tablespoon dry sherry
1 tablespoon soy sauce
2 cans (6½ ounces *each*) crabmeat, drained and flaked
8 green onions with tops, finely chopped
2 stalks celery, finely chopped
1½ pounds large shrimp, shelled and deveined
½ cup all-purpose flour
3 eggs
3 tablespoons milk
2 to 3 cups soft bread crumbs (from 8 to 10 bread slices)
Vegetable oil for frying

1. Heat 2 tablespoons oil in small saucepan over medium heat. Add yellow onion; cook and stir until tender, about 3 minutes. Add curry powder; cook and stir 1 minute. Add 1½ tablespoons sherry, satay sauce, 2 teaspoons soy sauce and sugar; cook and stir 2 minutes. Stir in cream; bring to a boil. Simmer 2 minutes, stirring occasionally. Keep warm.

2. Blend egg whites, cornstarch, 1 tablespoon sherry and 1 tablespoon soy sauce in medium bowl. Add crabmeat, green onions and celery; mix well.

3. Cut deep slit into, but not through, back of each shrimp.

4. Flatten shrimp slightly by pounding gently with mallet or rolling pin. Stuff crab mixture into slit of each shrimp.

5. Coat each shrimp lightly with flour.

6. Beat eggs and milk with fork in shallow bowl until blended. Place each shrimp, stuffed-side up, in egg mixture; spoon egg mixture over shrimp to coat completely.

7. Coat each shrimp with bread crumbs, pressing crumbs lightly onto shrimp. Place shrimp in single layer on cookie sheets or plates. Refrigerate 30 minutes.

8. Heat oil in wok or large skillet over high heat to 375°F. Add four or five shrimp at a time; cook until golden brown, about 3 minutes. Drain on paper towels. Serve with sauce. *Makes 4 servings*

Step 3. Slitting back of shrimp.

Step 4. Stuffing shrimp.

# Fried Rice

3 cups water
1½ teaspoons salt
1½ cups uncooked long-grain rice
4 slices uncooked bacon, chopped
3 eggs
⅛ teaspoon pepper
3 tablespoons vegetable oil, divided
2 teaspoons minced fresh ginger
8 ounces Barbecued Pork (page 22), cut into thin strips
8 ounces shelled deveined shrimp (page 74), cooked and coarsely chopped
8 green onions with tops, finely chopped
1 to 2 tablespoons soy sauce
Fresh chervil leaves for garnish

1. Combine water and salt in 3-quart saucepan; cover. Bring to a boil over medium-high heat. Stir in rice. Reduce heat to low; cover. Simmer until rice is tender, 15 to 20 minutes; drain.

2. Cook bacon in wok or large skillet over medium heat, stirring frequently, until crisp; drain.

3. Remove all but 1 tablespoon bacon drippings from wok.

4. Beat eggs with pepper in small bowl. Pour ⅓ of egg mixture into wok, tilting wok slightly to cover bottom.

5. Cook over medium heat until eggs are set, 1 to 2 minutes. Remove from wok.

6. Roll up omelet; cut into thin strips.

7. Pour ½ tablespoon oil into wok. Add ½ of remaining egg mixture, tilting wok to cover bottom. Cook until eggs are set. Remove from wok; roll up and cut into thin strips. Repeat with another ½ tablespoon oil and remaining eggs.

8. Heat remaining 2 tablespoons oil in wok over medium-high heat. Add ginger; stir-fry 1 minute. Add rice; cook 5 minutes, stirring frequently. Stir in omelet strips, bacon, pork, shrimp, onions and soy sauce. Cook and stir until heated through. Garnish, if desired.

*Makes 6 to 8 servings*

Step 2. Cooking bacon.

Step 4. Tilting wok to cover bottom with egg mixture.

Step 6. Cutting omelet into strips.

# Cold Stirred Noodles

**Dressing**
- 6 tablespoons soy sauce
- 2 tablespoons sesame oil
- 1/4 cup red wine vinegar
- 2 1/2 tablespoons sugar
- 1/4 to 1/2 teaspoon chili oil

**Noodles**
- 1 pound Chinese-style thin egg noodles
- 1 tablespoon sesame oil
- 1/2 large thin-skinned cucumber
- 2 small carrots
- 1 bunch radishes
- 3 cups bean sprouts
- 1 cup matchstick strips Barbecued Pork (page 22), optional
- 4 green onions with tops, cut into 2-inch slivers
- Thin cucumber slices for garnish

1. For dressing, combine soy sauce, 2 tablespoons sesame oil, vinegar, sugar and chili oil in small bowl; mix well.

2. Cut noodles into 6-inch pieces.

3. Cook noodles according to package directions until tender but still firm, 2 to 3 minutes; drain. Rinse under cold running water; drain again.

4. Combine noodles and 1 tablespoon sesame oil; toss lightly to coat. Refrigerate until ready to serve.

5. Cut cucumber into 3-inch pieces. Shred with hand shredder or food processor; set aside. Repeat with carrots. Shred radishes; set aside.

6. Add carrots to saucepan of boiling water; cook 30 seconds. Drain. Rinse under cold running water; drain again. Repeat with bean sprouts.

7. To serve, place noodles on large platter. Top with shredded cucumber, carrots, bean sprouts, radishes and Barbecued Pork; sprinkle with onions. Garnish, if desired. Serve with dressing.    *Makes 6 to 8 servings*

Step 2. Cutting noodles.

Step 5. Shredding cucumber.

Step 6. Cooking bean sprouts.

# Fried Noodles

8 ounces Chinese-style thin egg
    noodles
Salt
Vegetable oil for frying

1. Cook noodles according to package directions until tender but still firm, 2 to 3 minutes; drain. Rinse under cold running water; drain again.

2. Place several layers of paper towels over jelly-roll pans or cookie sheets. Spread noodles over paper towels; let dry 2 to 3 hours.

3. Heat oil in wok or large skillet over medium-high heat to 375°F. Using slotted spoon or tongs, lower a small portion of noodles into hot oil. Cook noodles until golden brown, about 30 seconds.

4. Drain noodles on paper towels. Repeat with remaining noodles. *Makes 4 servings*

Step 3. Frying noodles.

Step 4. Draining cooked noodles.

# Steamed Rice

1 cup uncooked long-grain rice
2 cups water
1 tablespoon oil
1 teaspoon salt

1. Place rice in strainer; rinse under cold running water to remove excess starch. Combine rice, 2 cups water, oil and salt in medium saucepan.

2. Cook over medium-high heat until water comes to a boil. Reduce heat to low; cover. Simmer until rice is tender, 15 to 20 minutes. Remove from heat; let stand 5 minutes. Uncover; fluff rice lightly with fork.

*Makes 3 cups*

Step 2. Fluffing rice.

# Vermicelli

**8 ounces Chinese rice vermicelli**
***or* bean threads**
**Vegetable oil for frying**

1. Cut bundle of vermicelli in half. Gently pull each half apart into small bunches.

2. Heat oil in wok or large skillet over medium-high heat to 375°F. Using slotted spoon or tongs, lower a small bunch of vermicelli into hot oil.

3. Cook until vermicelli rises to top, 3 to 5 seconds; remove immediately.

4. Drain vermicelli on paper towels. Repeat with remaining vermicelli.

*Makes about 4 servings*

Step 1. Separating vermicelli.

Step 2. Adding vermicelli to hot oil.

Step 3. Cooking vermicelli.

# INDEX

Almond Chicken, 68
Asparagus Chicken with Black Bean
    Sauce, 64

**Bacon** (*see* **Pork**)
**Bamboo Shoots**
    Almond Chicken, 68
    Braised Shrimp with Vegetables, 74
    Combination Chop Suey, 72
    Mu Shu Pork, 52
    Seafood Combination, 84
Barbecued Pork, 22
Batter, 20
**Bean Curd:** Ma Po Bean Curd, 30
**Beef**
    Beef with Cashews, 46
    Beef with Peppers, 48
    Mongolian Lamb, 42
    Satay Beef, 38
Braised Lion's Head, 34
Braised Shrimp with Vegetables, 74
**Broccoli**
    Braised Shrimp with Vegetables, 74
    Chinese Vegetables, 26
    Hoisin Chicken, 56

Carrot curl garnish, 72
Carrot flower garnish, 38
**Chicken**
    Almond Chicken, 68
    Asparagus Chicken with Black Bean
      Sauce, 64
    Chicken Chow Mein, 62
    Chicken with Lychees, 66
    Chinese Chicken Salad, 70
    Combination Chop Suey, 72
    Hoisin Chicken, 56
    How to Cut Chicken Chinese-Style, 55
    Kung Pao Chicken, 58
    Lemon Chicken, 60
**Chinese Cabbage**
    Braised Lion's Head, 34
    Combination Chop Suey, 72
    Mongolian Lamb, 42
    Pot Stickers, 12
    Wonton Soup, 24

Chinese Chicken Salad, 70
Chinese Mixed Pickled Vegetables, 32
Chinese Vegetables, 26
Cold Stirred Noodles, 90
Combination Chop Suey, 72
**Crabmeat**
    Crab Sauce, 80
    Crab-Stuffed Shrimp, 86
    Fish Rolls with Crab Sauce, 80

**Fish**
    Fish Rolls with Crab Sauce, 80
    Seafood Combination, 84
Fried Noodles, 92
Fried Rice, 88

Green Onion Curls, 22

**Ham** (*see* **Pork**)
Hoisin Chicken, 56
Honey-Glazed Spareribs, 40
Hors d'Oeuvre Rolls, 15
How to Cut Chicken Chinese-Style, 55

Kung Pao Chicken, 58

Lemon Chicken, 60
Lemon Sauce, 60
Lo Mein Noodles with Shrimp, 78
Long Soup, 18

Mandarin Pancakes, 53
Ma Po Bean Curd, 30
Mongolian Lamb, 42
Mu Shu Pork, 52

**Pork**
    Barbecued Pork, 22
    Braised Lion's Head, 34
    Chicken Chow Mein, 62
    Combination Chop Suey, 72
    Fried Rice, 88
    Honey-Glazed Spareribs, 40
    Hors d'Oeuvre Rolls, 15
    Long Soup, 18
    Ma Po Bean Curd, 30
    Mongolian Lamb, 42
    Mu Shu Pork, 52
    Pot Stickers, 12
    Shrimp Toast, 10

Stuffed Mushrooms, 20
Sweet and Sour Pork, 44
Two-Onion Pork Shreds, 36
Vermicelli with Pork, 50
Wonton Soup, 24
Pot Stickers, 12

Red pepper curl garnish, 44
**Rice**
    Fried Rice, 88
    Steamed Rice, 92

Satay Beef, 38
**Sauces**
    Crab Sauce, 80
    Lemon Sauce, 60
    Sweet and Sour Sauce, 16
**Scallops**
    Scallops with Vegetables, 76
    Seafood Combination, 84
Scored cucumber slice garnish, 80
Seafood Combination, 84
**Shrimp**
    Braised Lion's Head, 34
    Braised Shrimp with Vegetables,
      74
    Chicken Chow Mein, 62
    Combination Chop Suey, 72
    Crab-Stuffed Shrimp, 86
    Fried Rice, 88
    Hors d'Oeuvre Rolls, 15
    Lo Mein Noodles with Shrimp, 78
    Seafood Combination, 84
    Shrimp Omelets, 82
    Shrimp Toast, 10
    Wonton Soup, 24
Steamed Rice, 92
Stuffed Mushrooms, 20
Sweet and Sour Pork, 44
Sweet and Sour Sauce, 16

Two-Onion Pork Shreds, 36

Vegetable bundle garnish, 15
Vermicelli, 93
Vermicelli with Pork, 50

Wonton Soup, 24

Zucchini Shanghai Style, 28